MW01680067

DISCOVERY GROUP

STUDENT GUIDE

Discipleship Series

CAMPUS CRUSADE FOR CHRIST

DISCOVERY GROUP STUDY GUIDE 1

DISCOVERY GROUP STUDY GUIDE

Published by Integrated Resources
100 Sunport Lane, Orlando FL 32809
ISBN 0-86605-134-1
IR Product No. 5011e

Printed in the United States of America.

DISCOVERY GROUP
LESSON 1

HOW TO BE SURE YOU'RE A CHRISTIAN

Our relationship with Christ can well be illustrated by three aspects of a marriage relationship.

For example:

- A man may be convinced **intellectually** that the woman who is his intended bride is the "right" one for him.
- He may be involved **emotionally** and love her with all his heart.
- But marriage requires more then the **intellect** and the emotions. It also involves the **will.**
- The man and the woman become husband and wife only when, as an act of their wills, they commit themselves to each other before a minister or other person of authority. The two words "I do" make the difference.

So it is in our relationship with Jesus Christ. It is not enough to believe intellectually in Christ. Nor is it enough to have an emotional experience. Though both are valid, you do not become a Christian until, as an act of your will, you receive Christ into your life as Savior and Lord.

The three elements that are important to both the marriage relationship and a relationship with Christ are: **Intellect, Emotion** and **Will.**

INTELLECTUAL COMMITMENT

Christianity is not a "blind leap of faith," but it is a personal relationship with God as He has revealed Himself through Jesus Christ. It is important for a person to have a clear intellectual understanding of who Christ is and what is involved in being a Christian.

Read John 10:30-33 and 14:6-9. List the claims that Jesus made about Himself in these passages.

According to Romans 1:4, what is the ultimate proof of Christ's claim to be God?

THE TRILEMMA POSED BY THE CLAIMS OF CHRIST

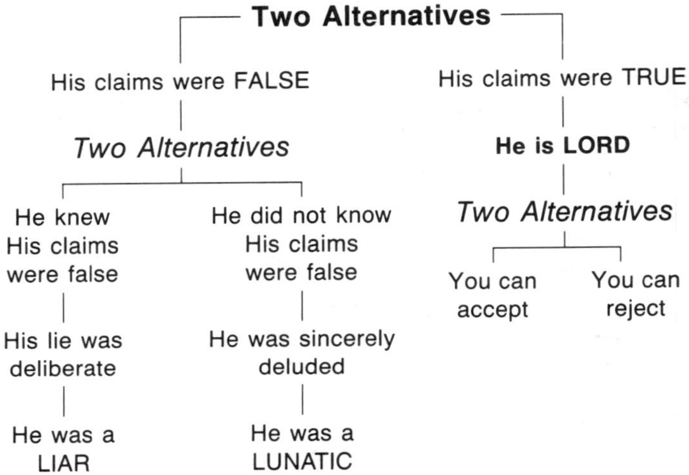

As you look at this chart, what would you say most students have concluded about Christ?

How did your thinking change about Christ? When?

EMOTIONAL COMMITMENT

Probably no one thing has caused more people to lack the assurance of a vital personal relationship with God through Jesus Christ than a wrong emphasis on emotions. Seeking an emotional experience contradicts faith- . . . the very thing that pleases God. The Bible says ". . . without faith it is impossible to please Him" (Hebrews 11:6).

Faith is another word for **trust,** and this trust must be placed in God and His Word rather than in what we might feel is true.

In what situations might you tend to trust in feelings rather than in God's Word?

VOLITIONAL COMMITMENT

In addition to the commitment of the intellect and the emotions, a commitment to Christ involves an act of the will. Though both mind and feelings are valid, you are not a Christian until, as an act of your will, you make a decision to accept Christ as Savior and Lord.

THE BASIS OF YOUR RELATIONSHIP WITH CHRIST

To begin a relationship with Christ you must understand several basic principles. . . what the message of the Gospel is, why we need the "good news," and what happens when we respond to it.

1. In 1 Corinthians 15:1-4, what is the message of the Gospel that Paul proclaimed?

2. According to 1 Corinthians 15:3 and Hebrews 9:22, why did Christ have to die?

3. According to John 1:12, what happens when a person responds (intellectually, emotionally and volitionally) to the Gospel?

CONFIDENCE IN CHRIST

As Christians, we can be sure of our relationship with God because Christ has done everything necessary to secure that relationship for us. If our relationship with God was dependent on our own good works, we could never have assurance. We would never know if we had done enough to please God.

Read Ephesians 2:8 and 9 (printed below) to review how someone becomes a Christian, filling in the answers in the chart as you go:

FOR BY GRACE	What is grace? *unmerited favor*
YOU HAVE BEEN SAVED	From what are you saved?
THROUGH FAITH	What are some synonyms for faith? In what are we to have faith? (See Galatians 3:22,26)
AND THAT NOT OF YOURSELVES, IT IS A GIFT OF GOD NOT AS A RESULT OF WORKS	What are some works that people do to try to earn favor with God?
THAT NO ONE SHOULD BOAST	Why is boasting excluded from a relationship with God?

Now rewrite these two verses in words you would use in explaining these ideas to a friend.

Becoming a Christian involves turning to God from self (repentance) and trusting Christ to forgive your sins, come into your life and make you the kind of person He wants you to be. Just to agree intellectually that Jesus is the Son of God and He died on the cross for your sins is not enough. Nor is it enough to have an emotional experience. You receive Christ by faith as an act of the will.

GOD'S PROMISES TO ALL CHRISTIANS

What do these verses promise you as a result of your decision to trust in Christ?

Revelation 3:20

1 John 5:11-13

John 10:27-29

John 5:24

SUMMARY:

1. **Which truth in this lesson is most meaningful to you?**
2. **As a result of what we've discussed how can a person be sure of personal salvation?**

ASSIGNMENTS:

1. Review the verses in this session and preview the ones in Session 2 as you spend some time (about 15 minutes) reading the Bible and praying each day.
2. Read "How to Experience God's Love and Forgiveness," Transferable Concept, Book 2.

HOW TO BE SURE YOU ARE A CHRISTIAN

A Transferable Concept by Bill Bright

My experience in counseling students and laymen through the years since I met Christ personally has convinced me that there are thousands of good, faithful church-goers who have "received" Christ, but who are not sure of their salvation. Regardless of how hard they try and how disciplined their efforts to please God, they are still uncertain of their relationship with Him.

Why does this heartbreaking uncertainty exist among so many who genuinely want to know God and have sought Him for years? I am persuaded personally that for many people this lack of assurance is due simply to misinformation regarding who God is, the true meaning of the crucifixion and the resurrection, and what is involved in receiving Jesus Christ as Savior.

Could it be that you yourself are still unsure of your relationship with God even though you may have been reared in a Christian environment and have "believed" in Him and in his Son for years? If you were to die this very moment, do you *know* for sure where you would spend eternity? Do you have the assurance right now that the Lord Jesus is in your life and that you are a child of God?

Or perhaps you have only recently received Christ and are still not sure that anything has really happened—you have no assurance of your salvation and have serious misgivings about where you will go when you die.

If you are among the vast multitude who are still looking for God, the next few moments could well be the most important ones of your life.

Becoming a Christian involves receiving by faith the greatest gift ever offered to man—God's gift of love and forgiveness through Jesus Christ. Receiving Jesus Christ as Savior and following Him as Lord involves one's *intellect, emotions* and *will.*

INTELLECTUAL UNDERSTANDING

In order to become a Christian or to be sure that you are a Christian, you must have a clear *intellectual understanding* of what is involved. Christianity is not "a blind leap of faith." It is built upon historical fact, documented by centuries of scholarship and research. Many leading scholars have dedicated their lives to investigating the life, teachings, death, resurrection and influence of Jesus of Nazareth. As a result, we have more historical evidence documenting these events of His life than we have of the fact that Napoleon was defeated at Waterloo.

Jesus Christ claimed to be God. He said, "I and the Father are one."[1] "He who has seen Me has seen the Father."[2] To become a Christian you must honestly face these claims and believe intellectually that Jesus is God, that He died for your sins and was buried, that He rose again and that He wants to come into your life and be your Savior and Lord.

EMOTIONAL INVOLVEMENT

Being sure that you are a Christian also involves the *emotions.* An emotion is a feeling or reaction to a specific act, event or experience. The failure to distinguish between different types of emotions has caused many people to be confused in their relationship with God. Probably no one thing has caused more people to lack the assurance of a vital relationship with God through Jesus Christ than a wrong emphasis on emotions.

One person may be aggressively extroverted and highly emotional, while another may be calm, reserved and introspective. Viewing the same act or participating in the same experience, these two may respond quite differently—one with great joy and the other calmly.

Each person who receives Jesus Christ as his Savior and Lord will have a different kind of emotional experience. Paul met God through a dramatic encounter on the road to Damascus. Timothy, on the other hand, was raised in a Christian home where he came to know Christ at an early age and gradually grew in his faith. The fact that your experience with God may not be as highly emotional as that of someone else does not make it any less real. We must not depend on our emotions for they can be deceiving.

How, then, can one be sure that he is a Christian? Is there not some confirmation that God gives to the man who sincerely receives Christ? Scripture assures us of a threefold confirmation that Jesus Christ is in our lives and that we are children of God and have eternal life.

First, we have *the external witness of the Word of God.* Assurance is based on the authority of God's Word. When you meet God's conditions, as revealed in His Word, you can be assured that you are a child of God.[3] Second, there is *the internal witness of the Holy Spirit,* who "speaks to us deep in our hearts and tells us that we really are God's children."[4] Our changed lives are a third witness to the fact that we are Christians. "When someone becomes a Christian he becomes a brand new person inside. He is not the same any more. A new life has begun!"[5] This change may be sudden or gradual, according to the personality of the individual.

There *is* a place for emotions in the Christian experience, though we should not seek them nor attempt to recapture them from the past.

We are not to ignore the value of legitimate emotions. It is more important, however, to remember that we are to live by *faith*—in God and in His promises—and not by seeking an emotional experience. The very act of seeking an emotional experience contradicts the concept of faith, which is the only way to please God.

INVOLVEMENT OF THE WILL

In addition to the intellect and the emotions, becoming a Christian involves the *will.* Our relationship with Christ can well be illustrated by the requirements for a marriage relationship, which ideally must contain these same three ingredients—intellect, emotions and will.

For example, a man may be convinced intellectually that the woman who is his intended bride is the "right" one for him. He may be involved emotionally and love her with all his heart, but marriage requires more than the intellect and the emotions. It also involves the will.

It is not until the man and the woman as an act of the will commit themselves to each other before a minister or another person of authority that they become husband and wife. The two words "I do" make the difference. So it is in our relationship with Jesus Christ. It is not enough to believe intellectually that Jesus Christ is the Son of God and Savior of men, nor is it enough to have an emotional experience. Though both are valid, one does not become a Christian until, as an act of the will, he receives Christ into his life as Savior and Lord.

There may be a difference, however, between the marriage relationship and the Christian experience. In marriage the sequence of commitment is often intellect, then emotion and finally, will. But in commitment to Christ the sequence is usually: first, intellect, then will and, finally, as a by-product or result, emotions or feelings.

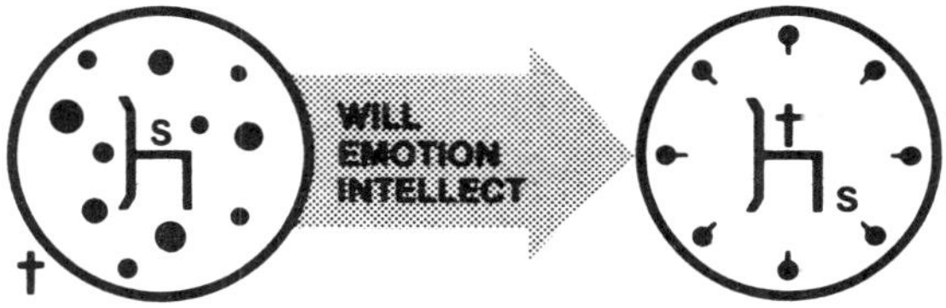

To be more sure that you are a Christian, you must be aware intellectually of certain basic scriptural truths:

First, God loves you and has a wonderful plan for your life.

Second, man is sinful and separated from God; thus he cannot know and experience God's love and plan.

Third, Jesus Christ is God's only provision for man's sin. Through Him you can know and experience God's love and plan.

And fourth, we must individually receive Jesus Christ as Savior and Lord; then we can know and experience God's love and plan.

Does this make sense to you? Have you ever personally received the Lord Jesus Christ as your Savior? If you have received Him, do you have the assurance of your salvation? Are you sure that, if you died right now, you would spend eternity with God in heaven?

If you cannot answer "yes" to these questions, may I suggest that you find a quiet place where you can be alone and receive the Lord Jesus as your Savior right now.

If you have never received Christ by a definite, deliberate act of your will, you can do so now in prayer. And if you are not sure you are a Christian, you can make sure now. In either case, may I suggest that you pray this or a similar prayer of faith, making it your very own.

"Lord Jesus, I need You. I thank You for dying for my sins. I open the door of my life and receive You as my Lord and Savior. Thank You for forgiving my sins. Take control of the throne of my life. Change my life and make me the kind of person you want me to be. Amen."

The decision to receive Jesus Christ as your Savior and follow Him as your Lord is absolutely the most important one you will make in your entire life.

1. John 10:30; 2. John 14:9; 3. John 1:12; 4. Romans 8:16, Living Bible; 5. II Corinthians 5:17, LB.

DISCOVERY GROUP LESSON 2

HOW TO EXPERIENCE GOD'S LOVE AND FORGIVENESS

About a year ago, Steve trusted Christ as his personal Savior. Things were going well for the first few months. He developed friendships with other Christians and had led several of his friends to Christ. He was enjoying his relationship with Christ and the security of his salvation. Then he began to notice that he was falling back into some of his old habits that he knew were not pleasing to the Lord. He tried to overcome those temptations, but with little success. He became aware that he no longer sensed the same warmth in his relationship with Christ that he had known earlier. The more he sinned, the worse he felt about it. Sometimes he wondered if his prayers were just bouncing off the ceiling. Eventually, Steve concluded that only "special" people could live an exciting, joyful Christian life. For most people, he thought, the Christian life was just a drag.

Why was Steve's relationship with Christ going cold?

In what ways can you identify with Steve's situation?

His struggles?

His feelings?

What do you usually do when you feel that way?

God has provided everything necessary for us to enjoy a dynamic, fulfilling relationship with Him. Unfortunately, the vast majority of Christians do not. In this lesson we will discover how to consistently experience God's love and forgiveness.

DESCRIBING THE PROBLEM: SIN

According to the Bible, there are three conditions of People. **Read 1 Corinthians 2:14-3:3.**

Natural (1 Corinthians 2:14)

- *has not trusted in Christ's death to pay for sin*

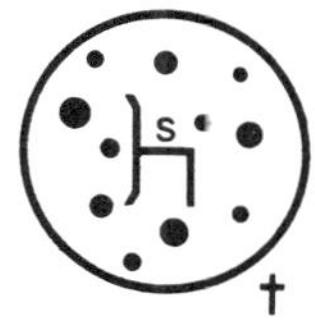

Natural

Spiritual (1 Corinthians 2:15)

- *has trusted in Christ's death to pay for sin*
- *allows Christ to direct the life*

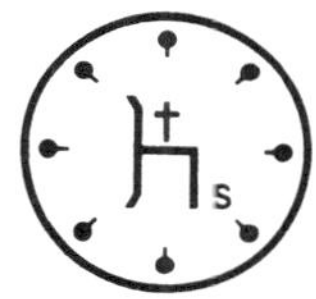

Spiritual

Carnal (1 Corinthians 3:1,2)

- *has trusted in Christ's death to pay for sin*
- *does not allow Christ to direct the life and relies on own efforts to life Christian life*

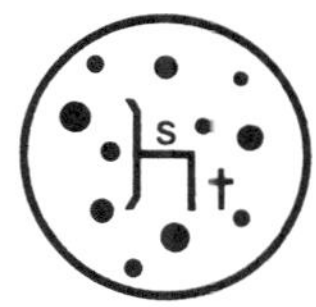

Carnal

What do you think determines whether a believer lives spiritually or carnally?

DEFINING THE PROBLEM: WHAT IS SIN?

Sin is the barrier which inhibits a carnal believer's experience of God's love and forgiveness.

Brainstorm as a group to write a good definition of sin:

Sin is any lack of conformity to the will of God—either an attitude or action. Any area of our lives in which we are not trusting God is sin. Most people think of sin as cheating, lying, immorality, etc. There are sinful acts that arise out of inward rebellion against Christ or simple indifference towards Him.

THE GREAT SOLUTION TO THE PROBLEM: JESUS CHRIST

Christ is God's only provision for sin. He has made it possible for believers to consistently experience God's love and forgiveness.

Read the passages in Hebrews 10 to see how God provided a solution to the sin problem:

QUESTIONS	OLD TESTAMENT HEB. 10:1-4	NEW TESTAMENT HEB. 10:10-18
Who was the mediator?	priest	Christ
How often was the sacrifice offered?		
Whose blood was shed?		
Was there a reminder of sin?		
Was the sacrifice sufficient?		

QUESTION AND ANSWER

1. **In light of your study in Hebrews 10, what is the basis for a Christian's forgiveness?**

2. **Read Colossians 2:13,14. How many of your sins were forgiven by Christ's death?**

3. **In the opening story about Steve, how could knowing he is totally forgiven make a difference in his life? In your life?**

So we see that your sins (past, present and future) are forgiven the moment you trusted Christ. But what do you do when you sin now?

DEALING WITH THE PROBLEM: SPIRITUAL BREATHING

You can experience God's love and forgiveness as you practice Spiritual Breathing, for just as you exhale and inhale physically, so you can exhale and inhale spiritually:

EXHALE: Confess your sins
INHALE: Appropriate the power of the Holy Spirit by faith

What does 1 John 1:8 say about the person who says he doesn't sin?

What does 1 John 1:9 say we are to do to experience God's forgiveness and cleansing?

CONFESSION involves at least three considerations:

1. Agree with God that a specific attitude or action is sin (CALL IT SIN).
2. Thank God that you are totally forgiven by Christ's death (CALL IT FORGIVEN).
3. Repent—change your attitude about sin by deciding to do what God wants you to do (CALL ON GOD TO CHANGE YOU).

AGREE OR DISAGREE?

1. God loves me more if I confess my sins.________
2. Confession enables me to experience what God has already said is true of me . . . He loves me and I'm forgiven.________
3. I should confess once a week for all known sin.________
4. I should confess as soon as I'm aware I have sinned so that God's power is not short circuited in my life.________
5 It's alright to commit sin since I've already been forgiven.__________

SUMMARY:

Your sin is totally forgiven because of Christ's death on your behalf. You can experience God's forgiveness and cleansing as you confess your sin.

ASSIGNMENTS

1. Write a list of any known sin the Holy Spirit brings to mind.
2. Write out 1 John 1:9 across the list and thank God for His forgiveness and cleansing by faith.
3. Destroy the list and make restitution when necessary.

Spend time each day reading God's Word and talking with Him. Reviewing these passages and thinking about their meaning will help you understand and apply the content of this session.

Suggested Scripture passages:

1 John 1
Psalm 21
Luke 7:36-50
Luke 15:11-32
1 John 4:7-12

HOW TO EXPERIENCE GOD'S LOVE AND FORGIVENESS

A Transferable Concept by Bill Bright

Jesus meant for the Christian life to be an exciting, abundant adventure. But most Christians do not know anything about this kind of life. To many the Christian life is a burden, a chore, a terrible cross to bear. They have never experienced the victory that Christ can give.

As I have had the privilege of speaking to thousands of Christians around the world in many lands, I have found that the average defeated, frustrated, fruitless Christian is not happy with his spiritual condition. He would like to change, but he does not know what to do. This kind of person does not need to be rebuked or criticized and condemned.

He knows he is headed in the wrong direction. He needs to be shown how to get turned around. He needs to understand the nature of his problem and how to find a solution to it. This is exactly what the Word of God provides for us.

In 1 Corinthians, Chapters 2 and 3, the apostle Paul, writing under the inspiration of the Holy Spirit, diagnoses the problem when he tells us that there are three kinds of people in the world—*the natural man, the spiritual man and the carnal man.*

SELF-DIRECTED LIFE
S - Self is on the throne
† - Christ is outside the life
• - Interests are directed by self, often resulting in discord and frustration

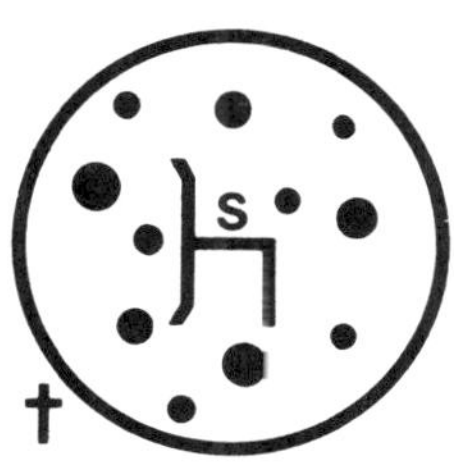

The natural man is not a Christian. He depends upon his own resources and lives in his own strength. He cannot understand or accept the truths of God's Word. His interests and ambitions are centered in things fleshly and worldly. Spiritually, he is dead to God—dead in trespasses and sin.

CHRIST-DIRECTED LIFE
† - Christ is in the life and on the throne
S - Self is yielding to Christ
• - Interests are directed by Christ, resulting in harmony with God's plan

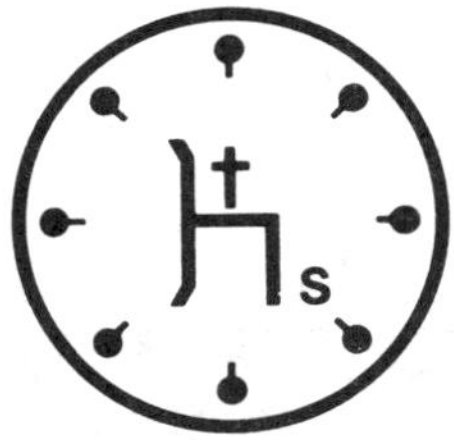

The spiritual man, however, is a Christian who is controlled and empowered by the Holy Spirit of God. He draws upon the unlimited resources of God's love and power and lives in the strength of the living Christ. He understands and believes God's Word, and his interests and ambitions are centered around and subject to the perfect will of God. Spiritually, he is alive. He is rejoicing in the Lord and bearing fruit for our Savior because he is allowing the Holy Spirit to have unhindered control of his life.

The carnal man, described by Paul in I Corinthians, Chapter 3, is a defeated and fruitless Christian. He is living in the energy of the flesh instead of drawing upon the inexhaustible resources of the Holy Spirit. He may be a Sunday school teacher, a salesman, a student, or even a minister or missionary who, even though he is a Christian, is in control of his own life—wanting to be his own master and hoping to please Christ at the same time.

SELF-DIRECTED LIFE
S - Self is on the throne
† - Christ dethroned and not allowed to direct the life
• - Interests are directed by self, often resulting in discord and frustration

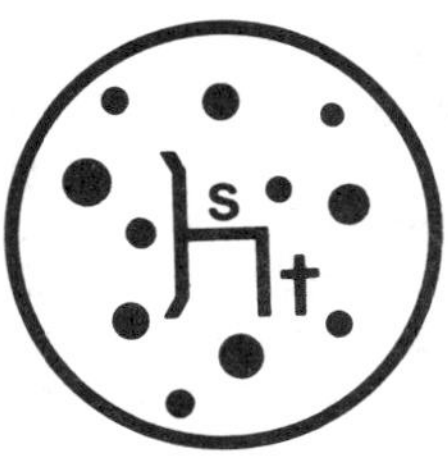

The carnal man desires and sometimes attempts to set his affection on the things of God,but still holds on to the things of this world. He may assume that he knows what God wants him to be and may honestly try to live up to that self-made standard, only to fail again and again, because of rebellion, lack of information on the role of the Holy Spirit, or lack of faith. He never allows the Holy Spirit to mold him into the person that God created him to be. Thus, in endless frustration, he lives outside the perfect will of God.

How well I remember the years when I sought God with all my heart. I resorted to all kinds of self-imposed discipline, begging God for His power. The more I tried, the more defeated and frustrated I became. Then one day, I was studying the book of Romans. I read Chapter 8, verse 7 (Living Bible): "The old sinful nature within us is against God. It never did obey God's laws and it never will."

What a relief it was for me to discover that I would never be able to live the Christian life through my own self-efforts. My only hope for victory, power and fruitfulness was to trust Christ to live His resurrection life in and through me. He and He alone could enable me to live the Christiian life.[1] It is faith, not effort, that pleases Him.[2]

OBJECT OF FAITH

What is faith? Faith is another word for trust. Faith must have an object. The Christian's object of faith is God and His Word. And His Word tells us that we need not continue to be defeated, carnal, fruitless and impotent Christians. We can be fruitful witnesses for Christ, and that is what He has called us to be.[3]

The Lord Jesus made the incredible but reliable promise that if we believe on Him, we will be able to do greater works than He did.[4] He assured us that whatsoever we ask in His name, He will do it.[5] No Christian need continue to be a carnal man.

It is important that we recognize that it is our Lord and Savior, Jesus Christ, the object of our faith, who has both the power and the willingness to deliver us from carnality.

We do not have faith in faith itself. For example, a person could have great faith that the ice on a lake would be thick enough to support his weight. Through his faith, he may walk boldly out on this ice and get very wet. On the other hand, a person who may have a very weak faith, may move slowly out onto a lake covered with a very thick layer of ice. As he walks on the ice and realizes its ability to support his weight, his faith grows.

So it is in the Christian life. We place our faith, even a faith that may be very weak, in a trustworthy God and His Word. The better we know God, the more we can trust Him, and the more we trust Him, the more we experience the reality of His love and grace and power. Faith is like a muscle—it grows with exercise.

PRACTICAL ATHEISTS

A man booked passage on a ship with just enough money to buy a ticket, a block of cheese and some crackers for a long voyage. The first few days at sea the crackers and cheese tasted good, but eventually they became stale. As he watched the porters carry large steaks, lobsters, chicken, beautiful salads and many other delicious foods to the other guests, he became so hungry that he finally stopped one of the porters.

"I'll do anything to get one of those steaks," he said. "I'll wash dishes, clean rooms, even mop the deck." The porter replied, "You bought a ticket, didn't you? The meals come with the ticket."

Too many people today are, ignorantly, cheese and cracker Christians —missing out on all of God's steak dinners.

It is tragically true that the average Christian is a practical atheist. He professes to believe in God, yet he acts as though God either does not exist or is unwilling to help him. All the resources of God are available to him, yet he lives in self-imposed spiritual poverty on a roller coaster of emotions. He fails to act as a child of the King or live as one who has been adopted into royalty from a state of poverty and illiteracy. How can the carnal man get off and stay off this emotional, roller coaster-type of existence and overcome his inconsistent way of life?

'SPIRITUAL BREATHING'

Consider the victorious fact stated by Paul in Colossians 1:13,14: "For He delivered us from the domain of darkness, and transferred us to the kingdom of His beloved Son, in whom we have redemption, the forgiveness of sins."

These verses, along with the message of Hebrews chapter 10, assure us: When we enter God's kingdom by receiving His Son, then we can experience, *moment-by-moment,* the inner peace and freedom of His merciful forgiveness!

"Spiritual breathing" is a principle which enables the believer to live a consistent Christian life. Just as we exhale and inhale physically, so we can also exhale and inhale spiritually.

We "exhale" when we confess our sins, and we "inhale" when we appropriate the fullness of God's Spirit by faith. (This article deals with spiritual exhaling. Next month, we shall consider the concept of spiritual inhaling, how to be filled with God's Spirit as a way of life by faith.) The Bible promises, according to I John 1:9, "If we confess our sins, He (God) is faithful and righteous to forgive us our sins and to cleanse us from all unrighteousness."

Confession (*homologeo* in the Greek) suggests agreement with God concerning our sins. Such agreement involves at least three considerations. First, I acknowledge or agree with God that my sin or sins, which should be named specifically, are wrong and therefore are grievous to Him. Second, I acknowledge or agree with God that He has already forgiven my sins—past, present and future—because of Christ's death on the cross. It is essential to realize that there is nothing that I can do that will add anything to what He has already done for me. Third, I repent, which means that I change my attitude toward my sins. Through the enabling power of the Holy Spirit, this will result in a change in my conduct.

Instead of doing what my old sinful nature wants me to do, I now do what God wants me to do.

SHORT-CIRCUITING GOD'S POWER

One day, as I was playing with my son, operating the controls of his electric train, the train suddenly stopped running. I could not figure out what was wrong. I took the train apart and put it back together. I pushed the plug in and out of the socket, but nothing happened. Then I discovered the problem—a tiny piece of metal, a "no left turn" sign, had fallen across the positive and negative rails, short-circuiting all the electrical power generated for the vast city of Los Angeles, so that the train would not run.

In like manner, sin short-circuits the power of God in the lives of Christians. God is holy and will have nothing to do with sin. But God loves us even though we may have unconfessed sins in our lives. He has forgiven us. All that we need to do to experience afresh the wonder of His love and the joy of His promises is to confess our sins—exhale spiritually—and experience the reality of His cleansing power.

Let me challenge you to perform a simple exercise now. Take a pencil and paper and list every sin in your life which the Holy Spirit calls to your remembrance. Take plenty of time; humble yourself before the Lord. Give God time to reveal to you those areas of your life which need to be corrected.

Meditate on Psalms 32:1-6, and pray the prayer of Psalms 139:23, "Search me, O God, and know my heart; test my thoughts. Point out anything you find in me that makes you sad . . ."

When you have written all that the Lord shows you to be wrong in your life, write across the list the wonderful promise of I John 1:9 quoted above. Now destroy your list and thank God for His forgiveness and cleansing through the shedding of His Son's precious blood for your sins.

As you learn to breathe spiritually, i.e., exhale—confess, or agree with God concerning your sin, whenever you grieve or quench the Holy Spirit; then, inhale—appropriate the power of the Holy Spirit on a moment-by-moment basis—you will experience true freedom and victory in the Christian life. Your life will become a great adventure, and you will become a fruitful witness for our Lord.

1. Colossians 3:10, Living Bible; 2. 1 Peter 1:7, LB; Hebrews 11:6; 3. John 15:16; 4. John 14:12; 5. John 14:14.

DISCOVERY GROUP LESSON 3

HOW TO BE FILLED WITH THE HOLY SPIRIT

Who is the Holy Spirit and Why Did He Come?

The Holy Spirit is God, the third person of the Trinity (God the Father, God the Son, God the Holy Spirit—one God who has always existed in three persons). When you received Christ, the Holy Spirit came to live in you.

In order to learn more about the Holy Spirit and what He does, match the Scripture references in the left column with the correct statements about the Holy Spirit:

John 14:16, 17	• Guides us in the truth of God's Word
John 16:8	• Convicts of sin
John 16:13	• A Helper
John 16:14	• Gives power to witness
Acts 1:8	• Glorifies Christ
1 Corinthians 3:16	• Assures us we are His children
Romans 8:16	• Indwells all believers

What Does it Mean to be Filled with the Holy Spirit?

Though all Christians are indwelt by the Holy Spirit from the moment of spiritual birth, not all are controlled or empowered by Him.

1. "To be filled with the Spirit is to be directed and empowered by Him."

What is the main difference between being filled with sin and being filled with the Holy Spirit?

2. "To be filled with the Spirit is to abide in Christ."

Read John 15:1-5

What comparisons can you draw between the relationship of the vine to a branch and of Christ to a Christian?

3. "To be filled with the Spirit is to bear fruit."

Read John 15:8

What are some specific changes you hope to see as God produces His fruit in you?

According to the following passages, what is the fruit that we are to bear?

Matthew 4:19; Galatians 5:22, 23; Ephesians 5:18-20

As the Holy Spirit controls us, we mature in Christ and the fruit of the Spirit becomes increasingly evident in our lives.

What are the characteristics of a Spirit-filled life?

God works to develop His fruit in the life of a person who is filled with the Holy Spirit.

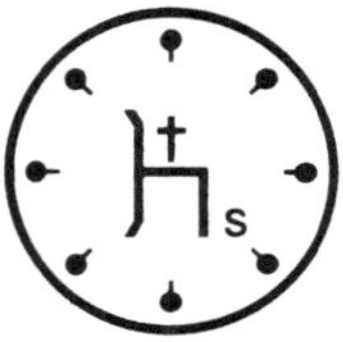

The following chart lists some of the qualities of a person who is filled with the Holy Spirit. Mark an X by those which you have been trusting God to develop within you:

____Christ centered	____love
____empowered by Christ	____joy
____witness	____peace
____obeys God	____patience
____effective prayer	____kindness
____understands Bible	____self control

The degree to which these traits are developed in a believer's life depends on the extent to which the Christian trusts the Lord with every detail of living and upon growth toward Christian maturity.

This diagram shows the life of a Christian who is trusting in personal efforts to live the Christian life. (The Bible calls this person "carnal.")

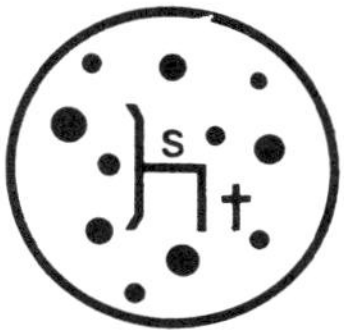

Christians get into this condition for two reasons:

1. Lack of Knowledge

2. Lack of Belief

Our previous lesson introduced an important discipline in the Christian life—*Spiritual Breathing.* Remember, to *exhale* is to confess sins. *Inhaling* is the obedience to God's command to be filled with the Holy Spirit.

Read God's command in Ephesians 5:18.

Read God's promise in 1 John 5:14,15.

A person is filled with the Spirit by trusting God to take control of every detail of life. This prayer is one way of expressing this:

> "Dear Father, I need you. I acknowledge that I have sinned against you. Thank you that you have forgiven my sins through Christ's death on the cross for me. I now invite Christ to take control of the throne of my life. Fill me with your Holy Spirit as you commanded me to be filled. Thank you for your promise to do this if I ask in faith. Thank you for taking control of my life and for filling me with your Holy Spirit."

What Should You Do Now?

Does the prayer on the previous page express the desire of your heart? Circle one:

Yes **Not sure** **No**

If yes, ask God to fill you with the Holy Spirit right now.

Has he fulfilled His promise?

How do you know?

ASSIGNMENTS:

1. During the week, repeat the process of spiritual breathing as necessary to abide in Christ: *Exhale* by confessing your sins as you become aware of them; thank God that He is faithful and just to forgive and cleanse you. *Inhale* by asking God to continue to fill you with his Spirit.
2. Read "How To Walk in the Spirit," Transferable Concept, Book 4.
3. Spend time each day reading God's Word and praying. These Scriptures will be particularly helpful this week:

   1 Corinthians 2:14—3:3
   Galatians 2:20
   Ephesians 3:14-21
   John 7:37-39
   Matthew 9:35-38

HOW TO BE FILLED WITH THE SPIRIT

A Transferable Concept by Bill Bright

During the depression a man named Yates owned a sheep ranch in West Texas. Because he did not earn enough money to make his ranching operation pay, Mr. Yates was in danger of losing his ranch. His family, like many others, had to live on government subsidy.

Day after day, as Mr. Yates grazed his sheep over those rolling West Texas hills, he was no doubt greatly troubled about how he would be able to meet his financial obligations. Then a seismographic crew from an oil company came into the area and told Mr. Yates that they felt there might be oil on his land. They asked permission to drill a wildcat well and he signed a lease contract.

At 1,115 feet they struck a huge oil reserve. The first well came in at 80,000 barrels a day. Many subsequent wells were more than twice as large. And Mr. Yates owned it all! The day he purchased the land he received the oil and mineral rights. Yet, he had been living on relief—a multimillionaire living in poverty. The problem? He did not know the oil was there. He owned it, but he did not *possess* it.

I do not know of a better illustration of the Christian life than this. The moment we become children of God through faith in Christ, we become heirs of God, and all of His divine supernatural resources are made available to us. Everything we need—including wisdom, love, power—to be men and women of God and to be fruitful witnesses for Christ is available to us. But most Christians continue to live in self-imposed spiritual poverty because they do not know how to appropriate from God those spiritual resources which are already theirs.

It is useless to try to live in our own power the kind of life God has commanded us to live. Our strength must come from the Lord! The Holy Spirit came to enable us to know Christ. When we receive Christ into our lives, we experience a new birth, and are indwelt by the Spirit. The Holy Spirit enables us to live and share the abundant life which Jesus promised to all who trust Him.

LACK OF FAITH

Many Christians are not filled with the Spirit because of a lack of knowledge. Unbelief keeps others from experiencing the abundant life. There are still other Christians who may have been exposed to the truth concerning the person and ministry of the Holy Spirit but who, for various reasons, have never been able to comprehend the love of God. They are afraid of Him. They simply do not trust Him.

Suppose, when my two sons were young, they had greeted me with these words: "Daddy, we love you and have decided that we will do anything you want us to do from now on as long as we live." What do you think would have been my attitude?

If I had responded to their expression of trust in me as many believe God will respond when they surrender their lives to Him, I would have taken my sons by the shoulders, shaken them, glared at them sternly and said, "I have just been waiting for this. I am going to make you regret this decision for as long as you live. I am going to take all the fun out of your lives—give away your toys and make you do all the things you do not like to do."

Many people believe that this is the way God will respond when they say, "Lord, I surrender the control of my life to You." They do not understand how much God loves them. Do you know what I would do if my sons came to me with such a greeting? I would put my arms around them and say, "I love you, too, and I deeply appreciate this expression of your love for me. It is the greatest gift which you could give me and I want to do everything in my power to merit your love and trust."

Is God any less loving and concerned for His children? No, He has proved over and over again that He is a loving God—our heavenly Father who cares deeply for His children. He is worthy of our trust.

FILLED BY FAITH

How can one be filled with the Holy Spirit? We are filled with the Spirit by faith. We received Christ by faith. We walk by faith. Everything we receive from God, from the moment of our spiritual birth until we die, is by faith. Do you want to be filled with the Holy Spirit? You can be filled right now, wherever you are, by faith.

You do not have to beg God to fill you with His Holy Spirit. You do not have to barter with Him by fasting, weeping, or begging or pleading. For a long time I fasted, prayed and cried out to God for His fullness. Then one day I discovered from the Scriptures that the "just shall live by faith."[1] We do not earn God's fullness. We receive it by faith.

Suppose that you want to cash a check for a hundred dollars. Would you go to the bank where you have several thousand dollars on deposit, place the check on the counter, get down on your knees, and say, "Oh, please, Mr. Teller, cash my check?" No, that is not the way you cash a check. You simply go in faith, place the check on the counter, and wait for the money which is already yours. Then you thank the teller and go on your way.

Millions of Christians are begging God, as I once did, for something which is already available—just waiting to be appropriated by faith. They are seeking some kind of emotional experience, not realizing that such an attitude on their part is an insult to God—a denial of faith, by which we please God. In Hebrews 11:6 we are told, "Without faith it is impossible to please God . . . ."

HEART PREPARATION

Though you are filled with the Holy Spirit by faith and faith alone, it is important to recognize that several factors contribute to preparing your heart for the filling of the Spirit.

First, you must hunger and thirst after God and desire to be filled with the Holy Spirit. We have the promise of our Savior, "Blessed are those who hunger and thirst after righteousness, for they shall be filled."[2]

Second, be willing to surrender your life to Christ in accordance with Paul's admonition in Romans 12:1, 2 (Living Bible): "And so, dear brothers, I plead with you to give your bodies to God. Let them be a living sacrifice, holy—the kind He can accept. When you think of what He has done for you, is this too much to ask? Don't copy the behavior and customs of this world, but be a new and different person with a fresh newness in all you do and think. Then you will learn from your own experience how His ways will really satisfy you."

Third, confess every known sin which the Holy Spirit brings to your remembrance and experience the cleansing and forgiveness which God promises in I John 1:9 (LB): "But if we confess our sins to Him, He can be depended on to forgive us and to cleanse us from every wrong. And it is perfectly proper for God to do this for us because Christ died to wash away our sins."

COMMAND AND PROMISE

There are two very important words to remember. The first is *command.* In Ephesians 5:18 (KJV) God commands us to be filled: "Be not drunk with wine, wherein is excess, but be filled with the Spirit." Not to be filled, controlled and empowered by the Holy Spirit is disobedience. The other word is *promise*—a promise that makes the command possible: "This is the confidence which we have before Him, that, *if we ask anything according to His will, He hears us. And if we know that He hears us in whatever we ask, we know that we have the requests which we have asked from Him."*[3]

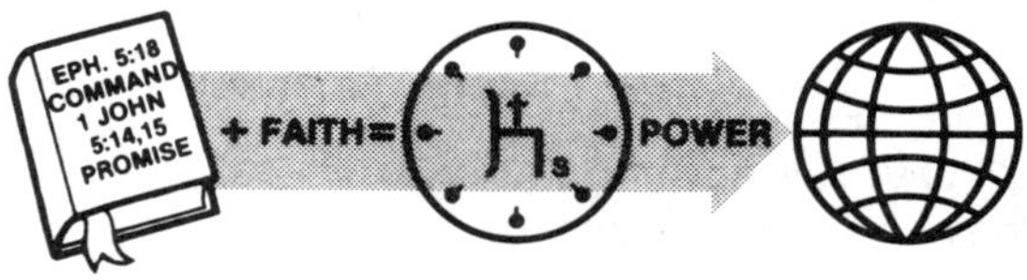

Now, is it God's will for you to be filled, controlled and empowered by the Holy Spirit? Of course it is His will—for it is His command. Right now, then, you can ask God the Holy Spirit to fill you—not because you deserve to be filled, but on the basis of His command and promise.

If you are a Christian, the Holy Spirit already dwells within you. Therefore, you do not need to invite Him to come into your life. The moment you received Christ, the Holy Spirit not only came to indwell you, but He imparted to you spiritual life, causing you to be born anew as a child of God. The Holy Spirit also baptized you into the body of Christ. In I Corinthians 12:13, Paul explains, "For by one Spirit we are all baptized into one body."

There is but one *indwelling* of the Holy Spirit, one *rebirth* of the Holy Spirit, and one *baptism* of the Holy Spirit—all of which occur the moment you receive Christ. There are many *fillings,* as is made clear in Ephesians 5:18. In the Greek language in which the New Testament was originally written, the meaning is clearer than in most English translations. This command of God means to *be constantly and continually filled, controlled and empowered with the Holy Spirit as a way of life.*

If you wish to be technical, you do not need to pray to be filled with the Holy Spirit, as there is no place in Scripture where we are told to pray for the filling of the Holy Spirit. *We are filled by faith.* However, since the object of our faith is God and His Word, I suggest that you pray to be filled with the Holy Spirit as an expression of your faith in God's command and in His promise. You are not filled because you pray, but because by faith you trust God to fill you with His Spirit in response to your faith.

Have you met God's conditions? Do you hunger and thirst after righteousness? Have you confessed every known sin in your life? Do you sincerely desire to be controlled and empowered by the Holy Spirit? If so, I invite you to bow and pray a prayer of faith right now. Claim the fullness of the Holy Spirit by faith:

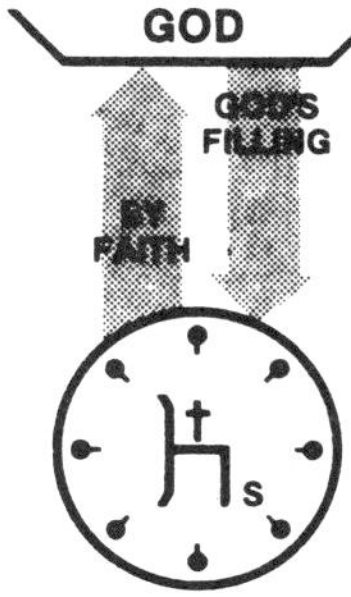

"Dear Father, I need You. I acknowledge that I have been in control of my life and that,as a result, I have sinned against You. I thank You that You have forgiven my sins through Christ's death on the cross for me. I now invite Christ to take control of the throne of my life. Fill me with the Holy Spirit as You commanded me to be filled and as You promised in Your Word that You would do if I asked in faith. I pray this in the authority of the name of the Lord Jesus Christ. As an expression of my faith, I now thank You for filling me with Your Holy Spirit and for taking control of my life."

If this prayer expressed the desire of your heart, and you met God's conditions of heart preparation, you can be sure that God has answered you. You are now filled with the Holy Spirit whether you "feel" like it or not. Do not depend on emotions—we are to live by faith, not feelings.

You can begin this very moment to draw upon the vast, inexhaustible resources of the Holy Spirit to enable you to live a holy life, and to share the claims of the Lord Jesus and His love and forgiveness with men everywhere. Remember that being filled with the Holy Spirit is a way of life. We are commanded to be constantly controlled by the Holy Spirit. Thank Him for the fullness of His Spirit as you begin each day and continue to invite Him to control your life moment by moment. This is your heritage as a child of God.

1. Galatians 3:11, King James; 2. Matthew 5:6; 3. I John 5:14,15.

DISCOVERY GROUP
LESSON 4

HOW TO WALK IN THE SPIRIT

WALKING IN THE SPIRIT DAY BY DAY

Indicate your thoughts about walking with Christ by responding to these Agree/Disagree statments (Mark "Yes" if you agree; "No" if you disagree):

____ To walk in the Spirit is to be free from difficulties.
____ A spiritually mature person can still sin.
____ A mature Christian is more spiritual than a less mature Christian.
____ A person must be a Christian many years in order to walk daily with the Lord.

DEALING WITH BARRIERS TO WALKING IN THE SPIRIT

Barriers arise in every Christian's life to prevent us from experiencing the fulfillment of God's promises:

The Barrier of Unconfessed Sin: 1) What it Does

Unconfessed sin is a barrier to walking in the Spirit. Sin will not affect our *relationship* with God. That is permanent—just as a child is permanently related to father and mother. However, sin will affect our *fellowship* with God.

Match either "relationship" or "fellowship" with the appropriate statements below:

Our Relationship with God is:

Our Fellowship with God is:

- restored by confessing sin
- maintained by God
- capable of being broken
- maintained in part by us
- eternally secure

The Barrier of Unconfessed Sin: 2) What to Do

As we learned in the previous two sessions, spiritual breathing is a means to deal with unconfessed sin.

EXHALE means. . .

Scripture:

INHALE means. . .

Scripture:

The Barrier of Self Effort

Read Romans 7:15-20

1. What is the source of Paul's struggle in this passage?

2. How did that make him feel?

3. When have you experienced similar frustration?

The Barrier of Circumstances

Many Christians allow both good and bad circumstances to sway their faith. However, the Christian is to live by faith, relying in the trustworthiness of God Himself and His word. The promise of God's Word, is our authority, not circumstances and our emotional responses to them.

This train diagram illustrates the relationship between **fact** (God and His Word,**faith** (our trust in God and His word), and **feeling** (the result of our faith and obedience, described in John 14:21).

Dealing with Barriers

1. From the past three lessons, what are some facts we can trust about God and our relationship with Him?

2. What is the outcome of placing our faith in each of these facts?

3. What would be the result in daily life of putting trust in these feelings instead of in God's Word?

4. In the chart below, list three areas of your life—classes, dating, sports, etc. Then describe how placing your faith in God's Word would affect each circumstance:

AREA OF LIFE	RESULT OF WALKING IN THE SPIRIT
1.	
2.	
3.	

Practicing Faith and Obedience

Walking in the Spirit is walking by faith in God and His Word. First, you must consciously decide to place your faith in God and His Word. Then you must obey. Obedience involves both confession of sin (1 John 1:9) and being filled with the Holy Spirit (Ephesians 5:18). It involves a daily commitment to allow Christ to live His life through you.

Walking in the Spirit is not:

a life of sinless perfection
a one-time "zap" of supernatural power
a life of constant "up" feelings
a mechanical formula

The following chart illustrates the difference between a life of self effort and a life of walking in the Spirit:

WALKING IN THE SPIRIT	Trusts in God and His Word	Experiences God's for-giveness through confession	Believes God to fill with His Spirit	God causes growth and fruit-fulness
WALKING IN SELF-EFFORT	Trusts in self ration-alization	Sin brings guilt or ration-alization	Increased effort to live by God's standards	Frus-tration and defeat

ASSIGNMENTS:

1. Read the following Scriptures during your daily time of prayer and Bible study:

   Colossians 1:27-2:10
   Ephesians 1:9-25
   Romans 6:1-18
   Romans 8
   Acts 4:9-25
   Colossians 1:9-12

2. Read "How To Witness in the Spirit," transferable Concept, Book 5.

HOW TO WALK IN THE SPIRIT

A Transferable Concept by Bill Bright

"Since I have learned how to walk in the fullness and power of the Spirit, the Christian life has become a great adventure for me," said a medical doctor after completing his third Lay Institute for Evangelism. "Now, I want everyone to experience this same exciting adventure with Christ."

Would you like to know how to experience a full, abundant, purposeful and fruitful life? You can! If you have been living in spiritual defeat—wondering if there is any validity to the Christian life—I have good news. There is great hope for you!

The Christian life, properly understood, is not complex nor difficult. As a matter of fact, the Christian life is so simple that we stumble over the very simplicity of it, yet it is so difficult that no one can live it! This paradox occurs because the Christian life is a *supernatural* life. The only one who can live it is our Lord Jesus Christ. It is only as we consistently abide in Him and walk in His Spirit that we will experience the abundant life with all that Christ means the Christian life to be.

How to walk in the Spirit through the practice of what I like to call "spiritual breathing" is a simple concept, but there are four very important factors which, rightly understood and applied, will contribute greatly to an understanding of this great adventure.

BE SURE YOU ARE FILLED

In order to walk in the Spirit, *we must first be sure that we are filled with the Spirit.* In Ephesians 5:18 (KJV), we are admonished, "Be not drunk with wine, wherein is excess; but be filled with the Spirit." To be filled with the Holy Spirit is to be controlled and empowered by the Holy Spirit moment by moment, as a way of life. We cannot have two masters.[1] There is a "throne," a control center, in every life—either self (ego) or Christ is on that throne.

We need to remember two important words: God's *command*—"be ye filled" *constantly and continually controlled and empowered*—by the Holy Spirit; and God's *promise*—if we ask anything according to God's will, He hears us, and if He hears us, He answers us.[2]

On the authority of God's command we know that we are praying according to His will when we ask Him to fill us. Therefore, we can expect Him to fill and empower us on the basis of His command and promise provided we genuinely desire to surrender the control of our lives to Christ, and trust Him to fill us. Technically, we are filled as an act of faith—not by asking to be filled—in the same way that we become a Christian by faith, according to Ephesians 2:8, 9 and not because we ask Christ to come into our lives.

Then continue to breathe spiritually, "exhaling" (confessing, then acknowledging God's love and forgiveness) whenever the Holy Spirit reveals a sin which you need to confess and "inhaling" (appropriating, by faith, the fullness and control of the Holy Spirit) as you continue to walk in the Spirit by faith.

WHAT ABOUT EMOTION?

Avoid being unduly introspective. Do not probe within yourself, looking for sin to confess. Confess only what the Holy Spirit impresses you to confess. Do not seek an emotional experience. If you genuinely hunger and thirst after God and His righteousness, and if you have confessed your sin, surrendered the control of your life to Christ and asked God to fill you, and you can *know* that you are filled with the Holy Spirit. Christ is now on the throne of your life. God will prove Himself faithful to His promise.

Do not depend upon feelings—the Christian is to live by faith, trusting in the trustworthiness of God Himself and His Word. This can be illustrated by a train diagram. Let us call the engine *fact*—the fact of God's promises found in His Word. The coal car we will call *faith*—our trust in God and His Word. The caboose we will call *feelings.*

It would be futile to attempt to pull the train by the caboose. In the same way we, as Christians, do not depend upon feelings or emotions. In order to live a Spirit-filled life we simply place our faith in the fact that God and His Word are trustworthy. Feelings will eventually follow in the life of faith,[3] but we should never depend on feelings or look for them. The very act of looking for an emotional experience is a denial of the concept of faith, and whatever is not of faith is sin.[4]

You can know right now that you are under the Holy Spirit's loving care by trusting in God, His command and promise, and you can go through life with that assurance.

SPIRITUAL CONFLICT

Second, *we must be prepared for spiritual conflict* if we expect to walk in the control of the Holy Spirit.

We are told in I Peter 5:7, 8 to let God have all of our worries and cares, for He is always thinking about us and watching everything that concerns us. We are to be careful watching out for attacks from Satan, our great enemy, who prowls around like a hungry roaring lion looking for some victim to tear apart. Satan is a real foe and we need to be alert to his cunning and subtle ways as well as to obvious attempts to defeat and destroy us. But we can have confidence knowing that "greater is He who is in you than he who is in the world."[5]

I once used this illustration to explain to a friend why he need not fear Satan. "What do you do with lions in your city?" I said. He replied, "We put them in a cage at the zoo." I said, "Visit the cage in the zoo and watch a lion pacing impatiently back and forth. He cannot hurt you. Even if you go up close to the cage, he still cannot hurt you if you are careful. But if you get in that cage the lion will make mincemeat of you. You have nothing to fear so long as you stay out of that cage."

Satan is in a "cage." Two thousand years ago Satan was defeated when our Lord Jesus Christ died on the cross for our sins. Victory is *now* ours. We do not look forward to victory but we move *from* victory—the victory of the cross. You have nothing to fear from Satan so long as you depend upon Christ and not on your own strength. Remember, Satan has no power except that which God in his wisdom allows him to have.[6]

KNOW YOUR RIGHTS AS A CHILD OF GOD

Third, if we are going to walk in the Spirit, *we need to know our rights as children of God.* We need to know how to draw upon the inexhaustible resources of God's love, power, forgiveness and abundant grace.

One of the most important things that we can do to learn about our rights as children of God is to spend much time in reading, studying, memorizing, meditating on the Word of God, and in prayer and witnessing. When Christ takes up residence in our lives, our bodies become temples of God. God's Word tells us that all authority in heaven and earth belongs to Christ[7] and we are complete in Him.[8] When we have Christ we have everything we need. Jesus promised special power to live holy lives and to be effective witnesses for Christ when we are controlled and empowered by Christ.[9]

At the same time we must remember that "the just shall live by faith."[10] Men think of *works* (Bible study, prayer and other spiritual disciplines) as the *means* to the life of faith. In truth they are the *results* of such a life.

LIFE OF FAITH

Fourth, if we are to walk in the Spirit, *we must live by faith.* It is sad to see wonderful, sincere Christians who have been deceived by a wrong emphasis on emotions. I know of nothing that has caused so much defeat and divisiveness among Christians. We do not live by feelings, but by faith. According to Hebrews 11:6, "Without faith it is impossible to please Him." In Galatians 3:11, Paul reminds us, "We live by faith."

In Romans 8:28 we find a promise of God believed by most Christians: "All things work together for good to those who love God, to those who are called according to His purpose." Do you believe this promise of God? If so, you logically acknowledge the reasonableness of the following command of God in I Thessalonians 5:18: "In everything give thanks; for this is God's will for you in Christ Jesus."

Have you learned to say, "Thank you, Lord," when your heart is broken because of the loss of a loved one? Do you thank God when your body is wracked with pain? When you receive a "Dear John" letter terminating a love relationship? When you have financial reverses?

You may say that only a fool would give thanks to God under such circumstances. No, not if all things work together for good for those who love God. If God has commanded us to give thanks, there is a reason for it. And let me tell you, as one who has some experience in this area this is one of the most exciting lessons that I have ever learned—the lesson of saying "thank you" when things go wrong, even when my heart is broken.

Why should a Christian desire to walk in the control of the Holy Spirit moment by moment? First, it is a command of God. Second, by continually yielding control of the throne of your life to Christ, you will please and honor Him, who delights to have fellowship with His children; you will enjoy a fuller, richer, more exciting life with our Savior and with others; and you will overflow with God's joy as your life becomes a witness for Him.

1. Matthew 6:24; 2. I John 5:14, 15; 3. John 14:21; 4. Hebrews 11:6; Romans 14:23; 5. I John 4:4b; 6. Acts 4:28; 7. Matthew 28:18; 8. Colossians 3:10; 9. Acts 1:8; Galatians 5:22, 23; 10. Romans 1:17, KJV.

DISCOVERY GROUP LESSON 5

HOW TO WITNESS IN THE SPIRIT

MOTIVATION FOR WITNESSING

There are four motivating reasons to share Christ with others:

1. LOVE FOR CHRIST

1. **According to 2 Corinthians 5:14-20, what motives dominated Paul's life?**

2. **What does an ambassador do for the one he or she represents?**

2. LOVE FOR PEOPLE

1. **According to Matthew 9:35-10:1, how did Jesus feel about the multitudes?**

2. **Why did He feel that way?**

3. **What did he do to demonstrate concern for the multitudes?**

4. **How would His view of people motivate you?**

3. PEOPLE ARE LOST WITHOUT CHRIST

1. **According to Ephesians 2:1-7, how did Paul describe the condition of a person who does not know Christ?**

2. **How does this motivate you to share Christ with people?**

4. DESIRE TO DO GOD'S WILL

1. **Read Matthew 28:18-20. What is the primary command of Christ in this passage?**

2. **What does Christ promise?**

Which of the four reasons given motivates you most strongly to want to share Christ with others?

Why?

THE MEANS FOR WITNESSING

Principle #1: Be sure you are a Christian.

Principle #2: Have no unconfessed sin in your life.

Principle #3: Be sure you are filled with the Holy Spirit.

These three principles of assurance in Christ and spiritual breathing were studied in the first four sessions. They are foundational to all Christian experience. This lesson applies them particularly to witnessing in the Spirit.

Principle #4: Be prepared to share your faith.

According to 1 Peter 3:15, what is required in order to be ready to represent Christ to others?

Practically speaking, how can you be ready to communicate to someone the importance of a relationship with Christ? List your ideas:

On a separate sheet of paper, briefly outline your account of the hope that is in you—your personal testimony. Include the following:

- What were you like before you trusted Christ?
- What were the details of your conversion (when, where, who led you to christ, etc.)?
- What happened in your life after your conversion?
- Where are you now in your relationship with Christ? Has made any specific changes in your life?

Be honest and straightforward without embellishment. Your testimony need not be dramatic to be used of God. It simply has to be the account of how God has worked in your life.

Principle #5: Pray.

It is not our wise words or smooth technique that cause a person to go from being "dead in our transgressions" to being "alive together with Christ" (Ephesians 2:1-6). Only the Spirit of God can cause that. By prayer, we have the opportunity to seek the Spirit's work in the lives of unbelievers.

Principle #6: Go.

Upon the foundation of Principles 1-5, we are then prepared to go. The gospel is to be shared with everyone. Jesus commissioned His disciples, including us, to take His message to the whole world (Matthew 28:18-20).

Principle #7: Focus on Christ.

As we go, we focus on Christ: who He is, His payment for sin and the eternal life He offers. We will not know the answer to every question a person might ask, but we can know that "God desires for all . . . to be saved" (2 Peter 3:9) and that God's Spirit is at work to draw people to Christ.

Principle #8: Expect results.

Because of God's Spirit being at work in people's lives, we can certainly expect results. Jesus has called us to fruitfulness (John 15:16). As a matter of fact, He has said, "the fields . . . are white for harvest!"

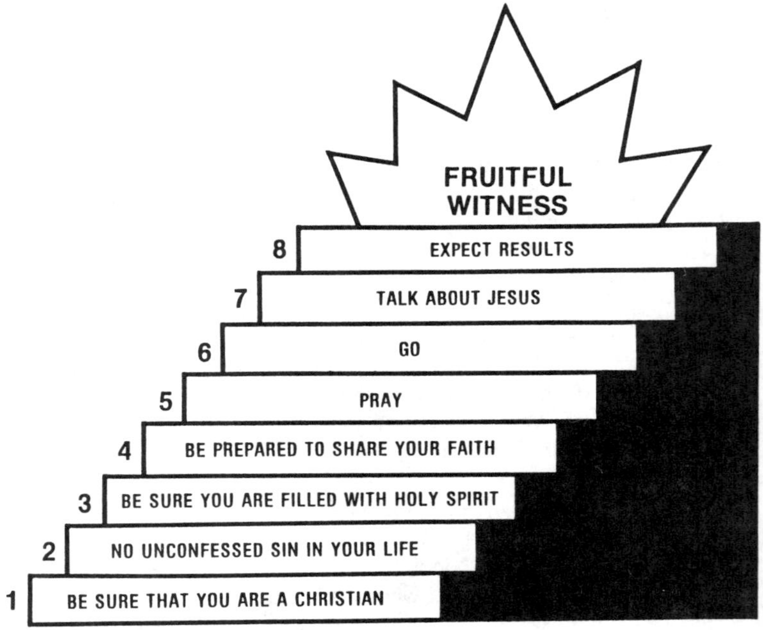

REVIEW OF WITNESSING – DO YOU AGREE OR DISAGREE?

____A Christian should be spiritually mature before telling someone about Christ.

____You can usually tell right away if a person will become a Christian.

____It is not necessary to answer all of a person's questions in order for that person to trust in Christ as Savior.

____Many people are ready to receive Christ the first time they clearly hear the gospel.

FOR FINAL CONSIDERATION:

Barrier: **What would be a barrier to keep a Christian from sharing the gospel?**

What can overcome that barrier?

Principles: What one or two principles seem to be the most important for you to remember in sharing your faith with others?

Why?

List five people you know for whom you can begin praying to come to know Christ:

1. ______________________________ 4. ______________________________

2. ______________________________ 5. ______________________________

3. ______________________________

ASSIGNMENTS:

1. Accompany group leader in sharing the good news this week at:
   (time) ______________________________

   (place) ______________________________

2. Read the following Scriptures:

   1 Timothy 2:1-7
   Romans 10:13-15
   2 Corinthians 5:14-21
   Romans 1:14-17
   1 Corinthians 2:1-5

HOW TO WITNESS IN THE SPIRIT

A Transferable Concept by Bill Bright

There is no experience in life more exciting and spiritually rewarding than the adventure of sharing Christ with others. All over the world, I have asked two questions of thousands of Christians and the answers are always the same, no matter whom I ask.

The first question is, "What is the most important experience of your life?" "Knowing Christ as my Savior," is the inevitable answer. The second question is: "What is the most important thing that you can do to help another person?" Again, the answer is always the same: "Help him to know Christ."

I am sure that, if you are a Christian, you would give the same answers to these two questions. Yet, how sad it is that so few Christians are sharing Christ with others. If you are typical of the majority of Christians today, you probably have never introduced anyone to Christ. You would like to do so, however, and you know in your heart that this is what God has called you to do. What is the problem?

It is largely twofold. First, the average Christian does not know how to live a victorious, vital, Spirit-controlled life; and second, the average Christian does not know how to effectively communicate his faith in Christ to others.

SCRIPTURAL FORMULA

I want to share with you a scriptural formula that can change your life. I can assure you that, if you follow this formula, you will experience in abundant life and will be fruitful for God in a way that you have never before known.

First, you must *be sure that you are a Christian,* that you have invited Jesus Christ to be the Lord and Savior of your life. Second, *be sure that there is no unconfessed sin in your life* and third, *that you are filled with the Holy Spirit.*

Fourth, *be prepared to share your faith in Christ.* I thank God for the way He is using some of the theological seminaries, Bible schools and other such instructional Christian institutions, but you do not need to take long years of training before God can use you. Not everyone has the gift of evangelism. But every believer is called to "do the work of the evangelist."[1] All of us have the privilege and responsibility of being witnesses for our wonderful Lord Jesus. Christ's Great Commission in Matthew 28:18-20 is for all Christians.

You see, it is our responsibility to abide in Christ—to allow Him to have control of our lives, to walk around in our bodies, to think with our minds, to love with our hearts and to speak with our lips. When we do this, He is the one who changes the lives of men. We are to abide in Him as the branch abides in the vine and He will produce fruit through us. It is our responsibility to follow Christ. It is His responsibility to make us fishers of men.

Here on earth He has no lips but ours, no feet but ours and no hands but ours. God has chosen to use men, not angels, to reach the world for Christ and, if we are obedient, He will use us. We can count on it.

PRAY

Fifth, *pray.* The Bible tells us that God is not willing that any should perish, but that all should come to repentance.[2] In addition, we have the promise that, if we ask anything according to God's will, He hears us, and if He hears us, He answers us.[3] Now, do you want your loved ones, your friends and neighbors to come to Christ? Then make a prayer list. Begin to claim them for God. God will not contradict Himself. You have the authority and integrity of His Word.

Share your faith in Christ with your loved ones and friends in the power of the Holy Spirit and by faith thank God that He will draw them to Christ.[4] I have prayed for loved ones with whom I used to weep, as I pleaded with them to come to Christ. Then I realized that God was not willing that they should perish—that He loved them more than I did—and so I began to thank God in faith that they would become Christians.

That day has not yet come for some of them. But I no longer weep. I rejoice in the assurance that one day they will come to Christ. God has promised and he does not lie.

I do not suggest that everyone who hears the gospel will become a Christian. It is our responsibility to pray for men to come to Christ and to share Christ with them. God alone by His Spirit can produce faith in the hearts of men and change their lives. It is important to remember that only the spiritual man can expect God to answer his prayer for the salvation of loved ones and others.

TELL OTHERS

Sixth, *go tell others of Christ.* Do not wait for men to come to you. Go to them with the good news. One of the greatest problems we all face—

one of the great barriers in witnessing—is the problem of getting going. There are all kinds of excuses: "I am too busy," or "I am waiting for the Holy Spirit to lead me to someone." We need not wait for the Holy Spirit to "lead us." Our Lord Jesus Christ has already commanded us to go tell the good news to all men.

Seventh, *talk about Jesus.* Paul said, "Everywhere we go we talk about Christ to all who will listen."[5] Do not talk about peripheral matters, such as the weather, sports or business, except where necessary for the purpose of becoming acquainted and establishing rapport. Pray and expect God to enable you to introduce His Son into the conversation.

As you talk to men about the Savior, you will discover that many people are ready to receive Him the very first time you talk to them. Some may need to "ripen" a bit. Be prayerfully sensitive to those with whom you talk.

'RIPE FRUIT'

As a young lad I used to visit my uncle's peach orchard. We would always pick the ripe peaches, but leave the green ones. Two days later, we would return to the same trees and pick more ripe peaches. Every two days we would find yet more ripe ones. So it is in our witness for Christ. We need to be sensitive to people. There are those who are ready to receive Christ, ripe for harvest, and there are those who are not ready. These represent green fruit.

Do not argue with those who are not ready. Do not badger them, browbeat them, insult them, nor try to pressure them into "making a decision for Christ." Give them something appropriate to read, leave them with a prayer, talk to them later—as the Lord gives opportunity—but continue to look for the ripe ones. They are all around you. Thousands, yes millions, of people whose hearts have already been prepared by the Holy Spirit are waiting to receive Christ.

There are many people who express antagonism toward God—they want nothing to do with religion. But when we tell them about Jesus, they are responsive. A taxi driver in Australia said to me, "I gave up all religion in World War II. I want nothing to do with a God who allows people to kill each other."

"Wait a minute," I said. "You are accusing God for something for which man is responsible. It is the evil in man, his sin, that causes him to hate and steal and kill." I explained the difference between religion, which is man's search for God, and Christianity, which is God's revelation of Himself in Christ to man. As I talked to him about the person of Christ, this man's entire attitude changed. Soon he said that he would like to pray with me and receive Christ.

Always encourage those with whom you share to invite the Savior into their lives. We really haven't "evangelized" until we have given people a chance to respond to the gospel. If possible, use a tool such as the Four Spiritual Laws booklet. It will help make your presentation of the gospel simple and understandable and the one with whom you share can use the booklet to share with his loved ones and friends also. Thousands of new Christians are leading others to our Savior in this way.

Eighth, *when you talk about Jesus, expect men to respond*—not on the basis of positive thinking, but because of your confidence in God, His love, His sovereignty, His power and His promise that He is not willing that any should perish, but that all should come to repentance.

There are many Christians who approach others with a negative attitude: "You don't want to become a Christian, do you?" By their negative attitude they unintentionally inhibit others from expressing their need for Christ. Go with the expectancy that God has already prepared the hearts of multitudes who are eager to receive Christ and you will find that He really has.

I believe that one of the greatest lies of the centuries is the attitude among Christians that men do not want God. The Christian world has been deceived into thinking that men will not be responsive to the gospel of our Savior. After more than 20 years of sharing Christ with thousands of students and laymen, individually and in small and large groups, I can tell you that the Holy Spirit has created a hunger for God in the hearts of multitudes around the world.

However, they must be properly approached if we expect them to acknowledge their need and to receive Jesus Christ as their Savior and Lord. They do not want religion. Many of them do not want anythng to do with the church at this point. They are not interested in peripheral, spiritual things and religious ritual, but they *are* interested in Christ! If we, in love, confront men with the person of Christ in the power of the Holy Spirit, many will respond to His love and forgiveness.

Having stressed the importance of expectancy in seeking to introduce others to Christ, I would like to share with you a statement which we in Campus Crusade for Christ sincerely believe and strongly emphasize: *"Success in witnessing is simply sharing Christ in the power of the Holy Spirit and leaving the results to God."*

Do you believe that if you follow this scriptural formula you will consistently have the privilege of introducing others to Christ through your witness? I can assure you that following it will enable you and every Christian to be fruitful for God as a way of life. This life on earth offers no other adventure that can compare to that of sharing Christ with others.

1. II Timothy 4:5; 2. II Peter 3:9; I Timothy 2:4; 3. I John 5:14, 15; 4. John 6:44; 5. Colossians 1:28, Living Bible.

DISCOVERY GROUP
LESSON 6

BUILDING A RELATIONSHIP WITH GOD

Matthew 7:24-27 is an account in which Jesus illustrates a crucial factor in building a relationship with God. **Read the passage and fill in the chart below.**

	Has he heard God's Word?	Has he acted on God's Word?	Did the foundation last?
WISE MAN			
FOOLISH MAN			

What was the main difference between the wise and the foolish man?

What was Jesus trying to teach His disciples in this parable?

ESTABLISHING A FIRM FOUNDATION

MY RESPONSIBILITY:

1. Walk in the Spirit by

a. ______________________________ *(Psalm 139:23,24)*

b. ______________________________ *(Romans 12:1,2)*

2. ____(2 Timothy 2:15)

3. Be willing
to ____(James 1:22-25)

GOD'S PROMISE

1. ____(Philippians 1:6)

2. ____(Philippians 2:13)

3. ____(John 15:5)

FOUR BUILDING BLOCKS OF A GROWING RELATIONSHIP

1. BIBLE STUDY

The bible is often referred to as the "Word of God" because it contains what God has communicated about Himself. **List reasons why God's Word is so important, based on the following Scriptures and your own personal experience.**

II TIMOTHY 3:16,17

PSALM 119:11,105

It is important to understand the balance between the role of the Holy Spirit and the role of God's word. The Word of God is closed to us apart from the illumination given by the Holy Spirit, while the Spirit is hindered in speaking clearly His life-changing truth apart from God's Word.

2. *PRAYER*

Prayer is conversing with and praising God as our loving heavenly Father. The Bible gives us principles to follow in the practice of prayer. **Match the passages below with the correct principle:**

Philippians 4:6-7	Pray about everything
	Pray daily
Mark 11:24	Pray specifically
	Pray continually
I Thessalonians 5:17	Pray in times of crisis
	Pray expectantly

Which of these principles have you applied so far in your praying? Do these truths about prayer motivate you to spend time with your heavenly Father? Why?

3. *FELLOWSHIP*

Fellowship is spending time and doing things with others who love Christ. Hebrews 10:25 emphasizes the importance of meeting with other Christians. **Why is this so important? Why do we need each other?**

If you spend most of your time with non-Christians and very little of your time with Christians, it is obvious which group will have the greater influence on your life. **What are some ways you can be more deeply involved in the lives of other Christians?**

What is a "witness" in a court of law?

How does "witnessing" describe the act of sharing Christ with someone else?

Anyone who has a vital personal relationship with Christ can be a witness for Him. As our lives are filled with the presence of the Lord Jesus, we cannot help but share Him. A vital Christian life is contagious. **Read Romans 1:14-16. How did Paul describe his motivation to tell people about Christ?**

How do you think witnessing helps you to grow in your relationship with Christ?

Bible study, prayer, fellowship and witnessing are important elements in developing your relationship with God, but time is also a factor. *There are no short cuts:*

> *A student asked the president of his school whether he could take a shorter course of studies than the one prescribed. "Oh, yes" replied the president, "but then it depends on what you want to be. When God wants to make an oak He takes 100 years, but when He wants to make a squash He takes 6 months."*

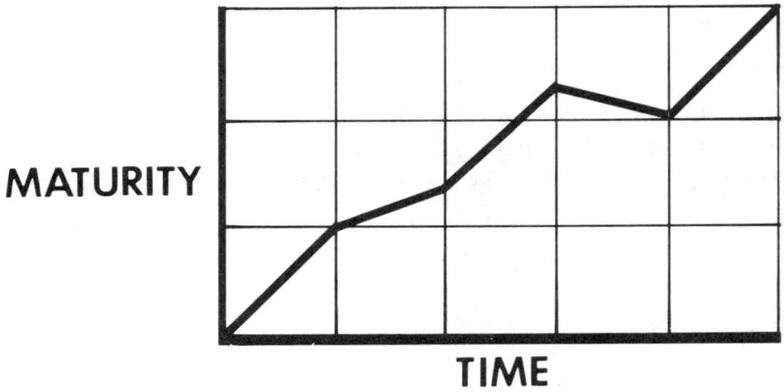

THINKING ABOUT GROWTH

1. How has this discovery group equipped and encouraged you to grow in your relationship with Christ?

2. Why do you want to continue being involved in growing in your relationship with God?

ESTABLISHING YOUR QUIET TIME WITH GOD

You can get to know God better through spending time alone with Him —reading His Word and conversing with Him in prayer. This is often referred to as a "Quiet time."

The primary purpose for a quiet time is to fellowship with our Father:

1. To concentrate on who God is as revealed in His Word.
2. To allow God to conform us to the image of Christ so that we bring glory to Him.

In your quiet time, concentrate on who God is rather than on what we're not. It pleases Him to see His children seek Him. As you focus your attention on God, you will be drawn closer to Him and see His character more clearly. It is crucial to develop an accurate view of God, and that comes through His Word.

These practical suggestions will help you have a rich and rewarding time with God:

1. Set aside a regular time each day to spend with God. Choose a time when you are alert. Give God your best time, not your sleepy or exhausted time.
2. Find a place where you can be alone, free from distractions.
3. Use a notebook to record prayer requests and things God is teaching you from His Word.
4. Use variety in your quiet time:
   a. Occasionally have your quiet time in a special place.
   b. Memorize several verses and ponder their implications for your life.
   c. Listen to Christian music to help you think about the Lord.
5. Spend time in the Word:
   a. Have a plan for your reading that will help you discover the exciting things God has for you throughout His Word.

b. Read slowly and thoughtfully.
c. Ask yourself questions about how the passage applies to your life.
d. Try reading a passage aloud.
e. Personalize Scripture by inserting your name in appropriate places and addressing the passage to God.

6. The word "ACTS" will help you talk to God.
   Adoration
   Confession
   Thanksgiving
   Supplication

   a. ADORATION: To adore God is to worship and praise Him. This is often done through song (Psalm 28:7) and through praying His Word back to Him (Psalm 103).
   b. CONFESSION: Tell God about the things you have done and said and thought which you know are wrong. He is faithful and just to forgive and cleanse you (I John 1:9). As you experience the forgiveness of sin, you will be free to fellowship with God.

      The vast majority of people in the world are burdened with guilt over past mistakes and sins. God's love and forgiveness lifts the burden of guilt, providing freedom to listen and respond to the Lord.
   c. THANKSGIVING: Thank God for all He has done, for all He is doing and for all He will do for you. Thank Him for the good and the bad things that happen to you, because He is sovereign and knows what is best for His children.
   d. SUPPLICATION: Pray specifically for your family, for others, and for yourself. Remember, specific prayer in accord with God's will yields specific results.

GETTING STARTED . . .

Use the space below to make a commitment to starting or continuing a quiet time:

1. I have set aside ________ as my regular time to meet with God.

2. I have picked ____________ as my regular place to spend time alone with my heavenly Father.

3. I will begin my study of the Word by reading ____________.

Some suggested Scripture for beginning a quiet time: John, Philippians, Colossians, Ephesians, I Timothy, I Thessalonians, I Peter, I John.

This book is the first step in three-part Discipleship Series.

THE DISCOVERY GROUP will help you understand the basics of living a positive and meaningful life.

It will help answer such questions as:

*How can my life be more effective and meaningful?
*Who is Jesus?
*How can I have a personal relationship with God?
*Should I have a personal relationship with God?
*Who is the Holy Spirit?
*Can I experience His Power?

ABOUT THE DISCIPLESHIP SERIES . . .

The DISCOVERY GROUP (Book 1) will help you understand the basics for living a victorious Christian life and how to begin to share your faith in Christ with others.

The DISCIPLESHIP GROUP (Book 2) will help you grow to a deeper level of spiritual maturity and learn more effective means of winning others to Christ and then guiding their spiritual growth.

The ACTION GROUP (Book 3) will help you teach others the biblical philosophy and methods for starting their own Discovery groups and Discipleship groups.

A Campus Crusade for Christ book
from Integrated Resources
100 Sunport Lane, Orlando, FL 32809

HOW TO INTRODUCE OTHERS TO CHRIST

A Transferable Concept by Bill Bright

"You must bring a lot of happiness into the world," said the young businessman with tears of joy and gratitude sparkling in his eyes. He had just prayed with me to receive Christ as his Savior. He and his wife had been looking for God for some time, he said, and now he was eager to take the Four Spiritual Laws booklet home with him so that he could in turn introduce his wife to Christ.

For more than 25 years I have had the exciting privilege of "bringing a lot of happiness into this world" by sharing the Lord Jesus Christ with thousands of students and laymen around the world.

One of the greatest misconceptions of the centuries is the idea so prevalent among Christians today—that men do not want God. Wherever I go I find ample proof that just the opposite is true. The Holy Spirit has created a hunger for God in the hearts of multitudes.

Yet, tragically, many Christians have never introduced anyone else to the Lord Jesus. Basically, there are two reasons for this. First, the average Christian is living a defeated, impotent, carnal life. He is not walking in the fullness and control of the Holy Spirit. Second, the average Christian has never been trained to communicate his faith in Christ effectively. He has never learned how to begin a conversation about Christ, how to explain the gospel simply and clearly, and how to lead a person to make a decision to receive Christ by faith.

THE KNOW-HOW

We cannot overemphasize the need for training in evangelism. "Know-how" often makes the difference between effective and ineffective witnessing. Basically, we witness in two ways; by the way we live and by the words we speak. We are specifically commanded to speak the good news with our lips, and that is the aspect of witnessing that we shall discuss here.

Before you can introduce others to Christ, however, there are certain things that you need to know: You must be sure that you are a Christian yourself. Then, as a Christian, you must know the empowering ministry of the Holy Spirit. You must also be sure of what people should know about God, Jesus Christ and the gospel before they can make intelligent decisions for Christ.

For many years, in our various student, lay and pastors institutes of evangelism, we used to ask those who participated in the training to help us list everything that they felt a person should know before he could make an intelligent decision for Christ.

Usually 25 to 50 different suggestions were made, all of which were written on the chalkboard. The list usually included the following:

God loves us.
Man is sinful.
Man is lost.
God loved us so much that He gave His Son.
Christ died for our sins.
Christ arose from the dead.
He wants to come into every life.
We must repent.
We must be born again.
We must receive Jesus Christ.
To as many as receive Him (Jesus), to them God gives the right to become His sons.

After all suggestions were exhausted, we ask each participant to read through the Four Spiritual Laws booklet with us and help us eliminate every point listed on the chalkboard that relates to Law One. These points were then removed from the board. We continued to Laws Two, Three and Four, following the same procedure. At this point, the chalkboard was always clean, for the distilled essence of the gospel is incorporated in the Four Spiritual Laws booklet.

We do not claim that use of the Four Spiritual Laws is the only way to introduce others to Christ, nor even the best way. However, we do know that tens of thousands of men and women have received Christ through the direct, simple presentation of the gospel contained in this booklet.

JUST GET STARTED

But even a Spirit-controlled person with a tested and trusted tool in his hands can expect barriers of resistance in sharing Christ with others. One of the most difficult barriers to overcome in witnessing is *just getting started.* No matter who you are or where you are, opportunities are always available. Assume that, whenever you are alone with another person for more than just a few moments, it is a divine appointment and an answer to your prayer.

There are many effective ways to establish contact. After a cordial, friendly greeting, you can say:

"Have you ever heard of the Four Spiritual Laws? This little booklet is one of the most widely read books in the world—approximately 100 million copies have been distributed in every major language of the world."

"The content of this booklet has changed my life."

"The content of this booklet has changed the lives of thousands. I would like to have you read it and give me your impression."

This direct approach can best be employed when you have only a few moments with an individual. If you have a more unhurried opportunity, you will want to take a few minutes to establish rapport by sharing a few things of personal interest about yourself and asking the other person about himself, his business, profession or family. Then you can proceed to explain that you are a Christian and that you have discovered a remarkable booklet that has been a great help to you and that you would like to share with him. Then ask, "Have you ever heard of the Four Spiritual Laws?"

As you prayerfully depend upon the Holy Spirit, He will give you wisdom in making the transition. However, no presentation will be effective unless God has already prepared the other individual's heart.

READ THE BOOKLET

When you share the gospel through the Four Spiritual Laws, do not elaborate with personal illustrations, which often confuse the one to whom you are speaking. Simply read through the booklet, but do not be mechanical. Be sensitive to the person's questions and needs. Keep in mind that you are introducing your friend or a stranger to our Lord Jesus Christ, the most wonderful person who ever lived.

Generally, it is wise for the one who is doing the witnessing to read aloud from the booklet, holding it at an angle so that the one with whom it is being shared can read along with him.

You will find that most people agree with the first three principles and are not likely to ask many, if any, questions. Thus you can proceed to Law Four with confidence. The material contained on pages 8 and 9 in the booklet will help you to determine whether a person is ready to receive Christ. You will observe two circles, one representing the self-controlled life, the other the Christ-controlled life. Ask the question contained in the booklet, "Which circle represents your life?" Then ask, "Which circle would you like to have represent your life?" In most cases the one with whom you are sharing will answer the first question, "The circle on the left," and the second question, "The circle on the right."

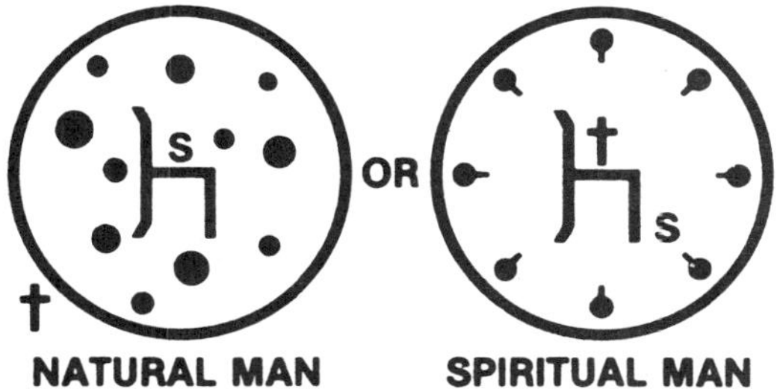

The next crucial point in sharing Christ is to help those who want to receive Him as their Savior to know exactly what to do. As you continue to read from the booklet, it will explain how one can receive Christ through a prayer of faith.

Read the prayer aloud and then ask, "Does this prayer express the desire of your heart?" If the answer is, "Yes," say, "You can pray this prayer right now if you really mean it, and Christ will come into your life as He promised." Then pause for prayer, with the suggestion that, if the individual would like to pray aloud, you can pray with him.

If there is a long silence, you may suggest that the individual pray after you. Be sensitive. Do not offend by "forcing" the prayer. He may wish to pray his own prayer rather than the suggested one. Should the individual wish to pray silently, suggest that he say "Amen" when finished. At this point, you pray.

NO RESPONSE?

If there is no commitment after you read the booklet through the first time to this point, exercise caution to avoid offending the one with whom you are sharing Christ. Do not try to badger, argue or high pressure him into making a "decision" for Christ. Jesus said, "No one can come to Me, unless the Father who sent Me draws him."[1]

The important thing is not what you do, but what the Holy Spirit does through you.[2] You and I do not have the ability to bring anyone to Christ. Remember that *success in witnessing is simply sharing Christ in the power of the Holy Spirit and leaving the results to God.*

Proper follow-up of the new Christian cannot be overemphasized. You should secure the name and address of each individual with whom you pray. This can be done tactfully and without offense if you give the person your name and address first. Then arrange to meet with the new Christian for spiritual counsel and follow-up not more than 48 hours later—the very next day if possible. If you can't meet personally, it will be helpful to the new Christian to receive a personal letter of encouragement and some helpful literature from you.

I challenge you to perform an experiment for the next 30 days. Each day, ask God to lead you to someone whose heart has been prepared for your witness. Go prayerfully and in the power of the Holy Spirit and, in the spirit of the apostle Paul, "talk about Christ to everyone who will listen."[3] Present the gospel as contained in the Four Spiritual Laws. Expect God to use you.

At the end of the 30 days, I am sure that you will be convinced, as multitudes of others have been before you, that there is no greater adventure in life than introducing others to our Savior. Remember, "you can bring a lot of happiness into this world" by sharing Christ with others.

1. John 6:44; 2. I Corinthians 3:6; 3. Colossians 1:28, Living Bible.